Newcomer ESL Workbook:
Phonics and Vocabulary Practice
With Real Photographs

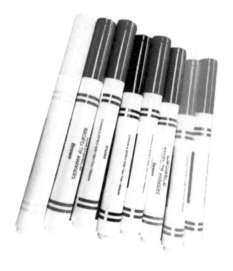

Newcomer ESL Workbook:
Phonics and Vocabulary Practice
With Real Photographs

Contact the author :
aworldoflanguagelearners@gmail.com

Table of Contents	Page
Instructions for Use	

Instructions for Use

Newcomer English Language Learners (ELLs) come with a range of vocabulary and phonics knowledge. Some students are literate in their home language, and others do not know how to read or write in any language. This workbook is designed to be used with newcomers at a range of beginning language levels.

Vocabulary Lessons
For students who are not yet literate in English, you will need to read the words from the vocabulary lessons to them.

Each lesson can be used first for speaking and then for writing.

Vocabulary Lessons for Speaking
Read the sentence frame to the student. Then, read the pictures above the sentence frame. Have students practice saying the sentence by adding in one of the picture words.

    I live in a <u>house</u>. by

<u>Matching:</u> Read a word to the student. Have the student point to the matching picture and repeat the word.

<u>Fill in the Missing Words</u>: Read the text to the student. Pause at the blank space and have the student point to and if they are able to say the missing word.

Vocabulary Lessons for Writing
Students choose one of the picture words to write on the blank line to complete the sentence.

<u>Matching</u>: Read a word to the student. Have the student draw a line from the word to the picture.

<u>Fill in the Missing Words</u>: Read the text to the student. The student write or glues in the missing words (at the back of the book are word cards for the missing words.
who

Instructions for Use

Phonics Lessons

Each phonics lesson introduces 2 or 3 English letters and the most common sound that letter makes (the sort vowel sound for vowels).

<u>Letter Introduction</u>: Write one letter on a whiteboard or show a letter flashcard (included in the back of the book). Say the letter name, the sound the letter makes, and key word that starts with that letter. Have students repeat after you.

 a, /a/, apple

<u>Beginning Sounds</u>: Say the name of each picture. Then, point to a letter and say its name and the sound that it makes. Have the student point to or circle the pictures that start with that sound.

 n /n/ What starts with the /n/ sound?

<u>Read Words</u>: The student reads the word and then points to the picture that shows the word.

<u>Write Words</u>: The student writes the word underneath the picture.,

<u>Read Sentences</u>: Students read the sentences. Then, where there are two pictures, they circle the picture that goes with the sentence.

<u>Spell Words</u>: Students spell the word that the picture shows. The letter or letters that make each sound go in each box. For sounds that have two letters, there are two lines inside the box; students write one letter on each line.

Decodable Lessons:

<u>Read</u>: The student reads the paragraph. There are labeled pictures to show the important words used in the text.

<u>Match</u>: The student reads a word and draws a line to the matching word.

<u>Write</u>: The student writes the missing words from the reading text. The missing words are the same words used in the matching section.

<u>Background Knowledge</u>: Read the fact sheet article to students. It gives additional information about the main topic of the decodable text. This helps to increase students' vocabulary knowledge and build their background knowledge.

My name is _____.

| apartment | house | townhouse | room |

I live in a/an _____.

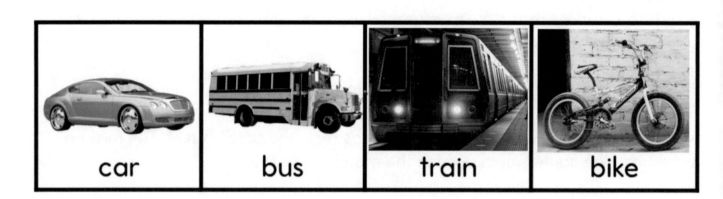

| car | bus | train | bike |

I ride in/on a _____.

walk | ride | run | sit

I can _____.

kid | teen | boy | girl

I am a _____.

school | the store | the playground | the library

I go to _____.

Match the nouns

house ●   ●

room ●   ●

car ●   ●

bus ●   ●

kid ●   ●

playground ●   ●

library ●   ●

Beginning Sounds

a	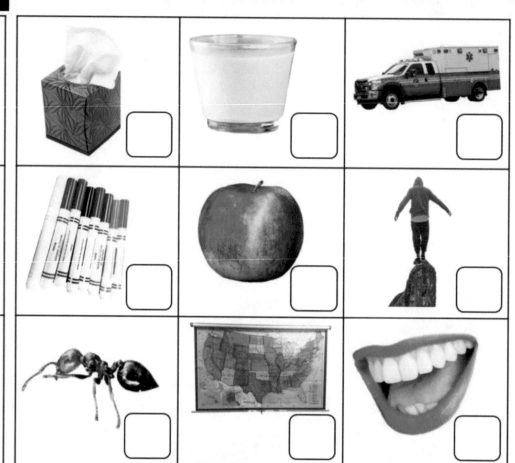
m	
t	

Read Words

Write Words

am

                    _____

mat

 _____

at

 _____

Read Sentences

I am at the bus stop.

I see a mat.

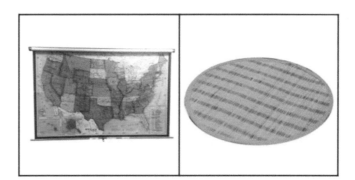

Spell Words

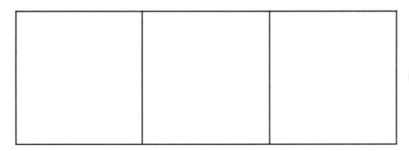

School

a book	newspaper	magazine	sign

I can read a _____.

crayons	markers	colored pencils	pens

I can draw with _____.

glue	tape	an eraser erase	a highlighter highlight

I use_____ to_____.

Fill in the missing words

School

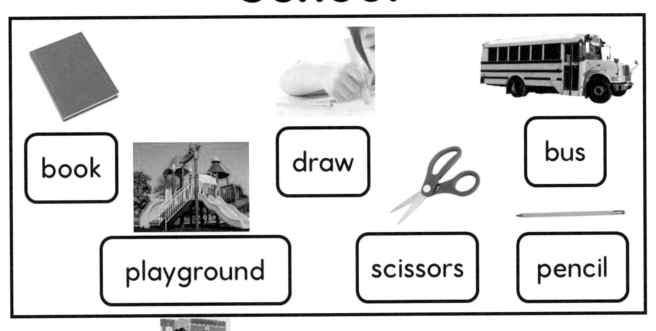

book draw bus

playground scissors pencil

I go to school on a ☐. I use a ☐

to read. In math, I use a ☐ to write

the answers. In art, I use markers to

☐ a picture. At school, I use ☐

to cut. At recess, I play on the

☐.

15

School

I go to school on a **bus**. I use

a **book** to read. In math, I use

a **pencil** to write the answers.

In art, I use markers to **draw**

a picture. At school I use

scissors to cut. At recess I

play on the **playground**.

Match the school supplies

book •

pencil •

markers •

glue •

crayons •

backpack •

©A World of Language Learners

Beginning Sounds

n	 ☐	 ☐	 ☐
p	 ☐	 ☐	 ☐
s	 ☐	 ☐	 ☐

Read Words **Write Words**

ant pan

_____ _____

tap map

_____ _____

sat nap
 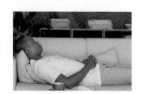
_____ _____

Read Sentences

I can tap the phone.

An ant is in the pan.

Spell Words

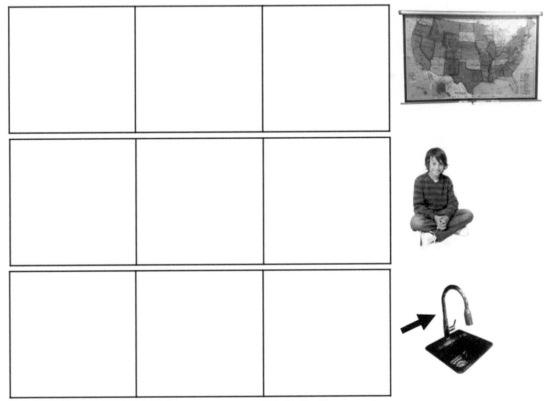

Read

The Ant

is on see sees the

I see a man.

The man sees an ant.

The ant is on a mat.

The man sees a pan.

The pan is on the ant.

The man can nap.

man	ant
mat	pan
on	nap

Match

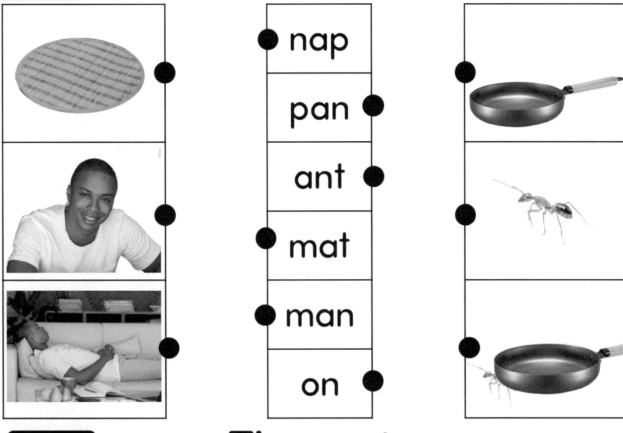

nap

pan

ant

mat

man

on

Write

The ant

I see a _____.

The man sees an _____.

The ant is on a _____.

The man sees a _____.

The pan is on the _____.

The man can _____.

Ants

An Ants Home

Ants live in a colony. There is a queen ant. The queen ant lays eggs. The eggs hatch into baby ants. The worker ants bring food to the queen ant. You can find ants inside or outside.

A queen ant with eggs.

Ants eating food.

Getting Rid of Ants

Most people do not like to find ants inside their home. People think that ants are a pest. People try different ways to get rid of ants. You can squish an ant. You can keep the inside of your house clean from food crumbs. You can also put out an ant trap.

You can squish an ant with your finger.

Keep your kitchen clean to help keep away ants.

An ant trap has poison inside of it. The ants eat the poison and bring it to the queen ant.

Numbers

1 one	2 two	3 three	4 four	5 five
6 six	7 seven	8 eight	9 nine	10 ten
11 eleven	12 twelve	13 thirteen	14 fourteen	15 fifteen
16 sixteen	17 seventeen	18 eighteen	19 nineteen	20 twenty

30 thirty	40 forty	50 fifty	60 sixty	70 seventy	80 eighty	90 ninety	100 one hundred

I am _____ years old.

How Many?

I see _____  bikes.

I see _____

 townhouses.

I see _____ trains.

I see _____

 buses.

Match the numbers

23 •

51 •

16 •

27 •

45 •

33 •

9 •

•
fifty-one

•
twenty-three

•
thirty-three

•
nine

•
forty-five

•
sixteen

•
twenty-seven

Beginning Sounds

i			
g			

Long or Short

I

 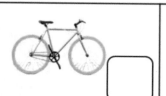 

Read Words

Write Words

in pig

_____ _____

pit tag

_____ _____

gas spin

_____ _____

Read Sentences

I can spin.

It has a pit.

Spell Words

Food

fruit

apple	grapes	bananas	berries

vegetables

			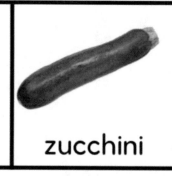
tomato	pepper	avocado	zucchini

grains

rice	bread	pasta	crackers

I like to eat _____.

I do not like to eat _____.

Colors

apple tomato pepper strawberry **red**	orange pumpkin carrot **orange**	bananas lemon pepper **yellow**
blueberries cupcake **blue**	grapes figs eggplant **purple**	cotton candy donut grapefruit **pink**
bread crackers cake ice-cream **brown**	zucchini olive avocado broccoli **green**	popcorn garlic cheese **white**

The _____ is/are _____.

food   color

Match the colors

red •

orange •

yellow •

blue •

purple •

pink •

brown •

green •

white •

•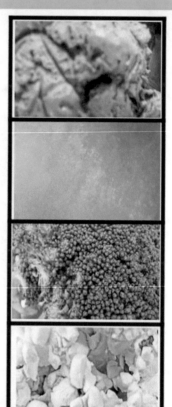

•

•

•

•

•

•

•

•

•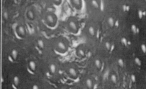

Beginning Sounds

d	desk ☐	tomato ☐	door ☐
k	kite ☐	key ☐	dog ☐

Ending Sound

ck	clock ☐	tissue ☐	stick ☐

Read Words

Write Words

stand dad _____

stick kick _____

mask kid

_____ _____

34

Read Sentences

The dads have a kid. The kid kicks a stick.

Spell Words

___ ___ ___ ___ ___ ___

The Cat

see the get gets

I see a cat.
The cat is in a sack.
A kid kicks the sack. The
cat is mad. Dad gets a
can. The cat gets a
snack.

kid

dad

cat	sack
kick	mad
can	snack

Match

kick

mad

can

snack

cat

sack

Write ## The Cat

I see a _____.
The cat is in a _____.
A _____ kicks the sack. The
cat is _____. Dad gets a
_____. The cat gets a
_____.

Cats

Boxes and Bags for Cats

Cats like to hide in boxes or bags. It helps the cat to feel safe. If a cat wants to be alone, it might go into a bag or a box. Cats like to be warm. The temperature inside most homes is too cold for a cat to be comfortable. A cat can go into a box or a bag to warm up.

A cat inside a box.

A sack is a type of bag. A sack is a large bag that usually has food inside. A cat can go inside a sack.

Bags and Cans of Food

Cat food can come inside a bag or a can. Most of the time, cat food inside a can is wet. Most dry cat food comes in a bag. Some cats only eat wet food. Some cats only eat dry food. Other cats like to eat both wet and dry food mixed together.

A can of wet cat food.

A bag of dry cat food.

| wake up | dressed | hair | breakfast |

In the morning I _____.

| learn | eat lunch | play | go home |

In the afternoon I _____.

| homework | eat dinner | brush my teeth | go to sleep |

In the evening I _____.

Fill in the missing words

Morning Routine

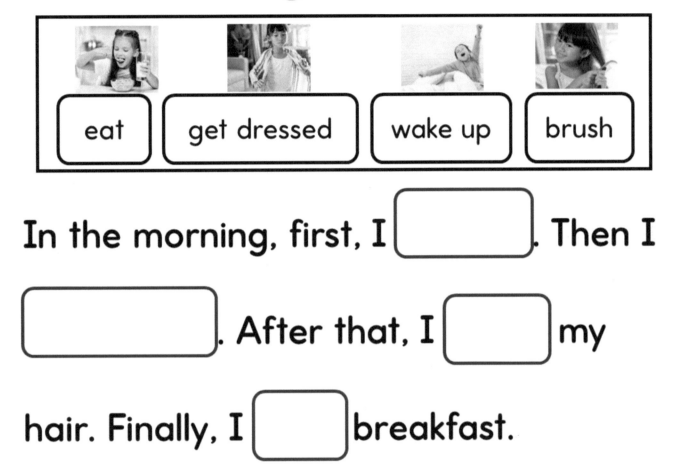

| eat | get dressed | wake up | brush |

In the morning, first, I [ ]. Then I

[ ]. After that, I [ ] my

hair. Finally, I [ ] breakfast.

Afternoon Routine

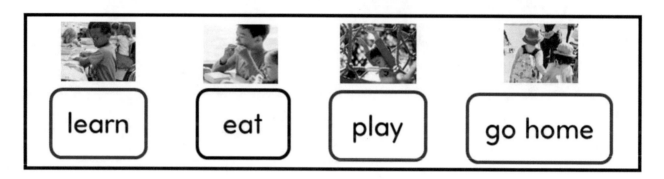

learn   eat   play   go home

In the afternoon, first, I ▢ at school.

Then I ▢ lunch. After that, I ▢

outside. Finally, I ▢.

Fill in the missing words

Evening Routine

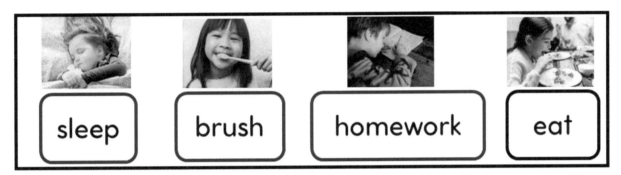

sleep   brush   homework   eat

In the evening, first I do my ⬚.

Then, I ⬚ dinner. After that, I ⬚

my teeth. Finally, I go to ⬚.

Morning Routine

In the morning, first, I wake

up. Then I get dressed. After

that, I brush my hair. Finally,

I eat breakfast.

Afternoon Routine

In the afternoon, first, I learn

at school. Then I eat lunch.

After that, I play outside.

Finally, I go home.

Evening Routine

In the evening, first I do my

homework. Then, I eat

dinner. After that, I brush

my teeth. Finally, I go to

sleep.

Match the verbs

eat ●   ●

brush ●   ●

learn ●   ●

play ●   ●

sleep ●   ●

Beginning Sounds

o		 ☐	 ☐
r	 ☐	 ☐	 ☐
h	 ☐	 ☐	 ☐

Read Words   **Write Words**

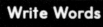 

hand top

_____   _____

stop pot

_____   _____

mom hat

_____   _____

Read Sentences

The mom has on a hat. I see a cat and a dog.

Spell Words

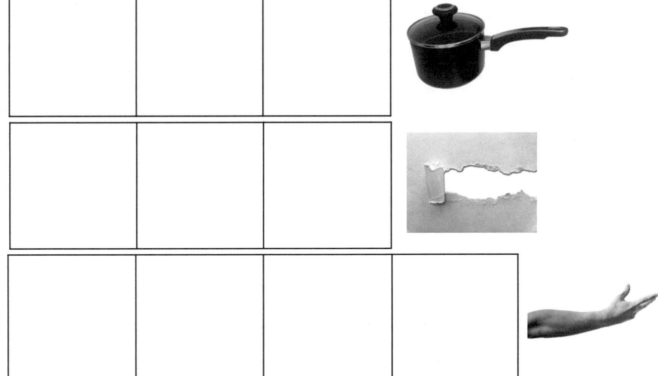

The Pig

from the have
my does

The pigs sip from mom pig. The pigs have a nap. I have a pig in my hand. The pig has a sip. The pig digs. The cat does not dig.

© A World of Language Learners

pig

nap

sip

hand

dig

cat

Match

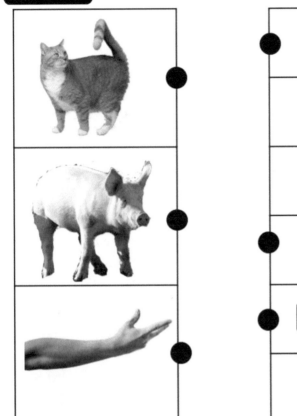

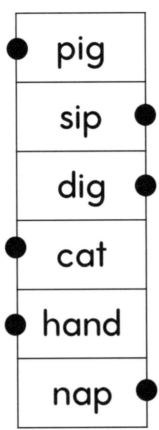

pig

sip

dig

cat

hand

nap

Write

The Pig

The pigs sip from mom
_____. The pigs have a
_____. I have a pig in my
_____. The pig has a
_____. The pig _____s.
The _____ does not dig.

Pigs

Baby Pigs

A mom or mother pig is called a sow. Baby pigs are called piglets. Piglets nurse from the mother pig. They get milk from her. Some piglets need help to get enough milk. A person can feed piglets milk with a bottle.

A person can feed a baby piglet with a bottle.

Piglets nurse from the mother pig to get milk.

Pigs that Dig

Pigs like to dig in the dirt. They dig to look for food. It is called rooting when a pig digs to look for food.

Pigs root or dig in the ground to look for food.

winter   spring   summer   fall

Weather

hot   cold   windy   wet

In the _____ it feels _____.
<small>season</small>   weather

Nouns

rain   snow   the sun   leaves

In the _____ I see _____.
<small>season</small>   noun

Hot

sunscreen	water	a hat	a shirt

When it is ____, I need _____.

Cold

a coat	a hat	gloves	a scarf

When it is _____ I wear _____.

Wet

a jacket	boots	umbrella	pants

When it is _____ I have _____.

Fill in the missing words

Winter

| snow | cold | hat | gloves |

In the winter, it feels ☐ I see ☐ outside. I wear a ☐ on my head. I wear ☐ on my hands.

Fill in the missing words

Spring

wet   boots   jacket   rain

In the spring, it feels ☐. I see ☐ outside. I wear ☐ on my feet. I wear a ☐ to stay dry (not wet).

Fill in the missing words

Summer

| sun | hat | hot | shirt |

In the summer, it feels ☐. I see the

☐ outside. I wear a sun ☐ on my

head. I wear a short sleeve ☐.

Fill in the missing words

Fall

coat | leaves | windy | rake

In the fall, it feels ⬚ . I see ⬚

outside. I wear a ⬚ to stay warm. I

use a ⬚ to rake the leaves.

Winter

In the winter, it feels **cold**. I see **snow** outside. I wear a **hat** on my head. I wear **gloves** on my hands.

Spring

In the spring, it feels **wet**. I

see **rain** outside. I wear **boots**

on my feet. I wear a **jacket** to

stay **dry** (not wet).

Seasons

In the summer, it feels **hot**. I

see the **sun** outside. I wear a

sun **hat** on my head. I wear a

short sleeve **shirt**.

Seasons

In the fall, it feels **windy**. I see

leaves outside. I wear a **coat**

to stay warm. I use a **rake** to

rake the leaves.

Match the clothes

shirt ●

pants ●

coat ●

hat ●

gloves ●

scarf ●

boots ●

●

●

●

●

●

●

●

Beginning Sounds

b	☐	☐	☐
l	☐	☐	☐
e	☐	☐	☐

Read Words

Write Words

bed red

bag pen

lick help

_____

_____   _____

_____   _____

_____   _____

Read Sentences

The bag is red.

The kid is sick in

bed.

Spell Words

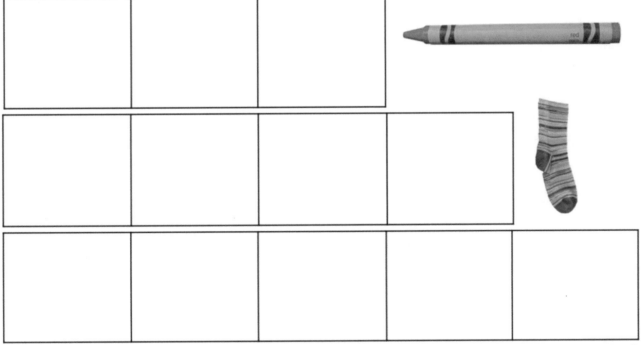

The Plant

the to see

The man gets a plant in his hand. The man digs.
The man plants the plant.
I see a gap to help the plants. The man can sit.
The plant will get big.

plant

sit

man

plant

hand

dig

gap

big

Match

| plant |
| man |
| hand |
| dig |
| gap |
| big |

Write

The Plant

The man gets a plant in his _____. The _____ digs.
The man plants the _____.
I see a _____ to help the plants. The _____ can sit.
The plant will get _____.

Plants

Plant: A Noun

A plant is alive. It has roots, stems, leaves, flowers, and seeds. Plants can grow in soil, sand, or water.

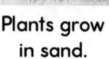

Plants grow in sand.

Plants grow in water.

Plants grow in soil.

leaves   seeds

stem

roots

flower

Replant a plant into the ground.

Plant seeds in a pot.

Plant: A Verb

You can plant seeds, a seedling, or a grown plant. You can plant seeds in a pot. Then when the seeds grow into a larger plant, you can replant it into a garden.

A garden has many plants. Leave a gap or space between the plants so each plant has room to grow.

Building

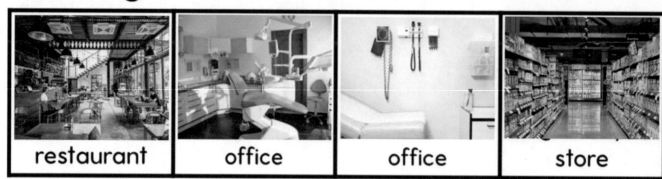

| restaurant | office | office | store |

Worker

| chef | dentist | doctor | cashier |

A _____ works at a _____.
    worker   building

Tools

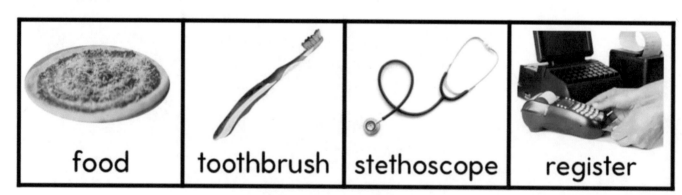

| food | toothbrush | stethoscope | register |

A _____ uses _____ at work.

Around the Community

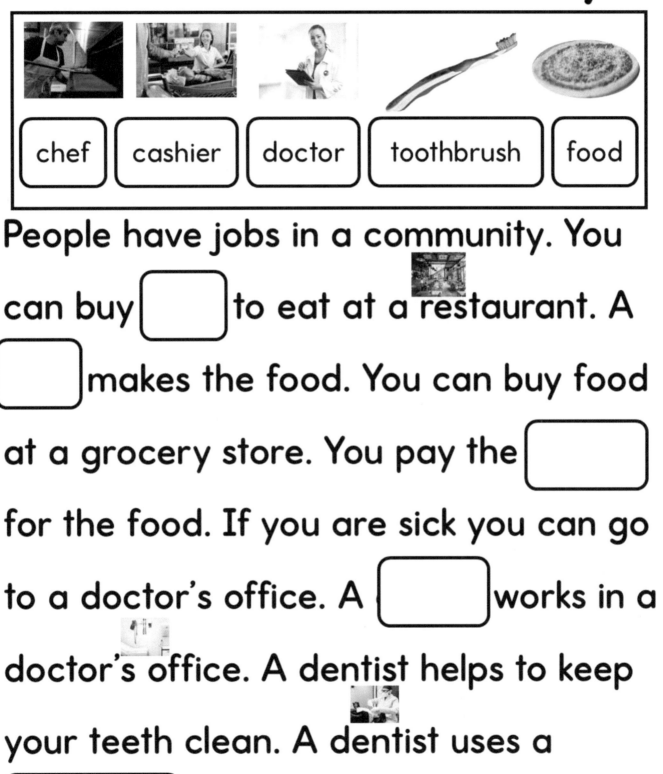

chef | cashier | doctor | toothbrush | food

People have jobs in a community. You

can buy ☐ to eat at a restaurant. A

☐ makes the food. You can buy food

at a grocery store. You pay the ☐

for the food. If you are sick you can go

to a doctor's office. A ☐ works in a

doctor's office. A dentist helps to keep

your teeth clean. A dentist uses a

☐.

Around the Community

People have jobs in a community. You can buy **food** to eat at a restaurant. A **chef** makes the food. You can buy food at a grocery store. You pay the **cashier** for the food. If you are sick, you can go to a doctor's office. A **doctor** works in a doctor's office. A dentist helps to keep your teeth clean. A dentist uses a **toothbrush**.

Match the nouns

grocery store ●

doctor ●

dentist ●

toothbrush ●

cash register ●

food ●

Beginning Sounds

f			
j			
w			

Read Words   **Write Words**

jet wig

win frog

fig jacket

Read Sentences

The wet dog is fast. The kids can spot a jet.

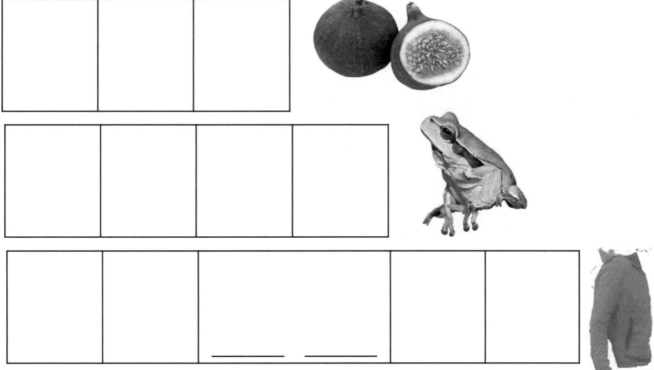

Spell Words

The Walk

her go of to the

Mom has a red jacket. Mom and her kid go on a walk in the fog. The kid stops and has a snack. The kid walks on top of a log. It is mom's job to help. The dog is in the back.

jacket	walk
fog	snack
log	dog

Match

jacket
fog
log
walk
snack
dog

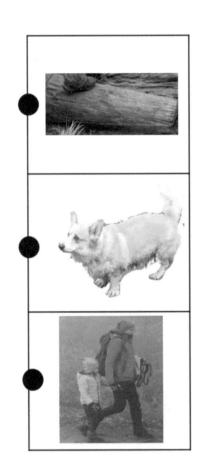

Write

The Walk

Mom has a red _____. Mom and her kid go on a _____ in the _____. The kid stops and has a _____. The kid walks on top of a _____. It is mom's job to help. The _____ is in the back.

A Hike

Where to Walk on a Hike

A hike is a walk in the woods. You can walk on a path. Sometimes you must walk over rocks or a log. There might be water under the rocks or under the log. It is important to be careful when walking on top of a rock or a log. You do not want to slip and fall.

You can walk on a path.

You can walk over a log.

You can walk on rocks.

The Weather on a Hike

You can hike in most types of weather. If it is cold, then you should wear a jacket. If it is foggy, you might have trouble seeing ahead of you. Walk slowly so that you do not trip. If it is hot, then you should bring extra water.

Fog is made up of water droplets. It can be hard to see through fog.

Take water on a hike.

Beginning Sounds

u	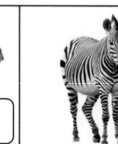 ☐	 ☐	 ☐
q	 ☐	 ☐	 ☐
z	 ☐	 ☐	☐

Read Words   **Write Words**

sun run

_____   _____

zip quiz

_____   _____

quilt hug

_____   _____

Read Sentences

Look at him dunk.

The man can run in the sun.

Spell Words

_____ _____			

Beginning Sounds

v	 ☐	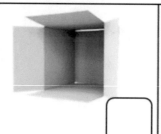 ☐	 ☐
y	 ☐	 ☐	 ☐

Ending Sound

x	 ☐	 ☐	 ☐

Read Words

Write Words

vet yes

box fix

van vest

_____   _____

_____   _____

_____   _____

Read Sentences

Mom helps the kid mix. The vet can help the dog.

Spell Words

The Gift

the onto
gives my

The kid wraps the gift. The kid gives her pal the gift box. In the box is a quilt. I hug my pal. I put the quilt onto my bed. My dog gets onto my bed.

pals

bed

wrap	give
gift box	hug
dog	quilt

Match

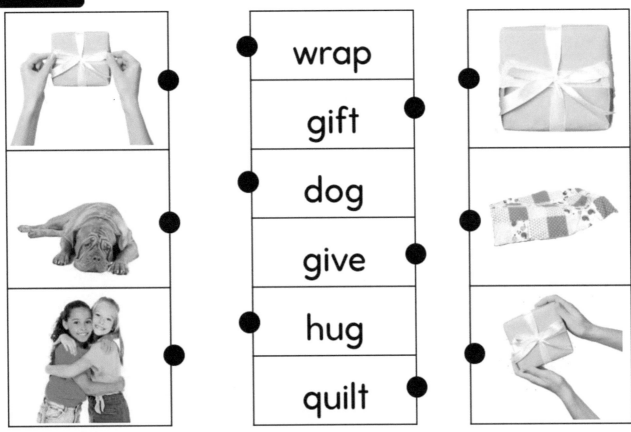

wrap	
gift	
dog	
give	
hug	
quilt	

Write

The Gift

The kid _____s the gift. The
kid _____s her pal the
_____ box. In the box is a
_____. I _____ my pal. I
put the quilt onto my bed. My
_____ gets onto my bed.

A Quilt

How to Make a Quilt

A quilt is a blanket. It is made by sewing pieces of fabric together. You can hand sew a quilt. You can use a sewing machine to make a quilt. Sometimes a group of people comes together to work on a quilt. This is called a quilting bee.

You can sew a quilt by hand. Use a needle and thread.

You can sew a quilt with a sewing machine.

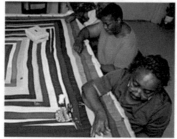

People work together to make a quilt at a quilting bee.

Where to Put a Quilt

A quilt can be used as a blanket on a bed. It helps to keep you warm. You can also put a quilt on the ground.

You can put a quilt on a bed.

You can put a quilt on the ground. A baby can play on top of the quilt.

Cut out the words and use to complete the missing word pages in the vocabulary sections.

2. School

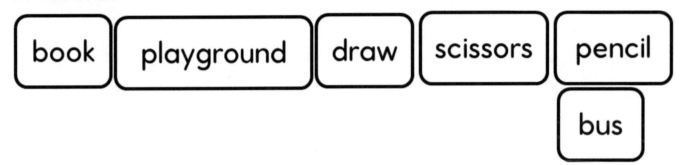

book | playground | draw | scissors | pencil

bus

5. Daily Routines

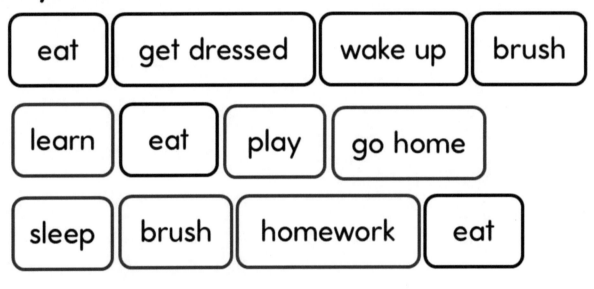

eat | get dressed | wake up | brush

learn | eat | play | go home

sleep | brush | homework | eat

Cut out the words and use to complete the missing word pages in the vocabulary sections.

6. Seasons

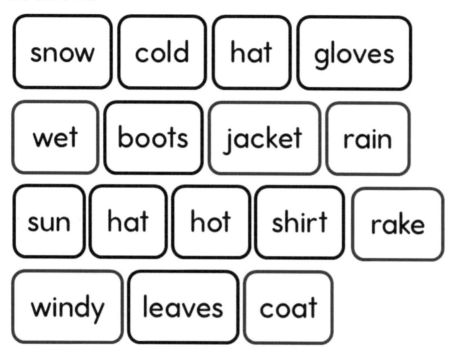

snow | cold | hat | gloves

wet | boots | jacket | rain

sun | hat | hot | shirt | rake

windy | leaves | coat

7. Around the Community

chef | cashier | doctor | toothbrush | food

Terms of Use

Thank you for purchasing this product.
The contents are the property of Ellie Tiemann and licensed to you only for classroom/personal use as a single user. I retain the copyright, and reserve all rights to this product.

You may not claim this work as your own, giveaway, or sell any portion of this product. You may not share this product anywhere on the internet or on school share sites.

Find more teaching resources at

https://www.teacherspayteachers.com/Store/A-World-Of-Language-Learners

Get weekly tips and find out about teaching resources at

https://www.aworldoflanguagelearners.com/newsletter/

Made in the USA
Columbia, SC
05 January 2025

51178821R00052